I am kind to myself.

I am kind to others.

I am enough
just as I am.

The characters and events portrayed in this book are fictitious or are used fictitiously.

Any similarity to real persons, living or dead, is purely coincidental and not intended by the author.

No part of this publication may be reproduced, stored in a retrieval system, or transmitted in any form or by any means, electronic, mechanical, digital, photocopy, recording, or otherwise except for brief quotations in printed reviews without the prior, written permission of the copyright owner.

The social-emotional content of this book is for informational and educational purposes only, and does not substitute professional medical advice, diagnosis, treatment, or consultations with healthcare professionals.

ISBN: 978-1-7360339-3-7

Library of Congress Control Number: 2022916129

Copyright 2023 by Carolyn Hunter

Written by Carolyn Hunter
Illustrated by Carolyn Hunter
Book published by Carolyn Hunter

Book design and layout by Caroll Atkins, Caroll Atkins Creatives

Printed in the USA

Cee Cee's Heart
Where Kindness Lives
ceeceesheart.com

"...Whatever is true, whatever is noble, whatever is right, whatever is pure,
whatever is lovely, whatever is admirable -
if anything is excellent or praiseworthy-think about such things."
Philippians 4:8

Dedication

I bestow the first fruits of my dedication, acknowledgment, and gratitude to God.

You are THE AUTHOR and THE PERFECTER of my faith.

Without You, I'd have no stories of kindness to tell.

I am so grateful that You entrusted me with such an

important message to help guard our children's peace of mind.

Foreword

When Carolyn Hunter asked me to write a Foreword for her book, I was thrilled, although I did not know her personally. As I listened to Carolyn discuss the contents of her book "Sometimes...Minds Get Boo-Boos, Too" with her Brand Stylist and book designer, my dear aunt Caroll Atkins, during a business meeting, I became intrigued. I curiously asked Carolyn to tell me more. Following a summary of her book, I was amazed at her creativity in crafting important mental health information into a story for children.

My name is Suzan Francis. I am a Licensed Clinical Professional Counselor, in the state of Maryland, a National Certified Counselor and a university professor for a Master of Arts program in counseling psychology. I hold a masters and a doctorate degree in counseling psychology. As a Psychotherapist, I am the owner of a clinical private practice, '**Lavi**' where I provide direct mental health assessments and treatment services to a diverse population of adults, couples, teenagers, children and families, across a full spectrum of mental health disorders.

This book satisfies my professional needs as a Psychotherapist who recognizes the general need for a book like this one in the mental health community. I love this book because the author manages to destigmatize talk and medication therapy for children in a fun, easy-to-understand manner. Parents who read this book to their children will help to create a safeguard for them to share their feelings, rather than internalizing and pathologizing. I particularly like that the book helps develop a child's emotional awareness; it helps create insight and brings clarity to children who do not know how to articulate bothersome thoughts and feelings. The contents will also help children learn that bothersome thoughts and feelings are normal. I think that it will be more effective if read to your child in order to help cultivate an atmosphere for open dialogue and sharing.

I am delighted that Carolyn, a passionate advocate for the mental wellness of children, included me in her journey of executing this lifelong goal. She recognized the need for such a book from 26 years as a requisite childcare provider. I have added this bibliotherapy to my practice for all young clients to benefit from the knowledge and wisdom of her words, carefully arranged to broadcast a powerful message. This book is a necessary read!

Counseling and Therapy

Empower & Transcend

Dr. Suzan Francis, EdD, LCPC, NCC
LaviMentalHealth.com
therapy@lavimentalhealth.org

Preface

The recent perilous and unprecedented events of our time have emphasized the world's tailspin, leaving the mental fortitude of few, if any, unchallenged. Sadly, our children have not been spared from the stress, many of whom are afraid to share their mind's troubles for fear of rejection and/or ridicule from peers and adults alike. Reports of mental illness events in children are increasing, and no child should ever suffer in silence. Every child is entitled to grow up in a safe, nurturing, and inclusive environment. A child's afflictions, including mental health problems, should be met by a tribe of trustworthy adults equipped with a responsive action plan of protective care, dignity, and reassurance. Children's reluctance to disclose mental health challenges is my call to action, the catalyst for the words and illustrations poured from my heart and pen to create "Sometimes…Minds Get Boo-Boos, Too." This Easy Reader children's book for ages 5-9 addresses the need to normalize children's mental health and wellness. The book is reliably narrated by Hannah's closest companion and my canine Kindness Influencer, "MacKzie," who joins me in inspiring Kindness on our growing Facebook page, "A Message From MacKzie." MacKzie shares the story of Hannah's mental health journey of obstacles and triumphs and relays an empowering message of hope, encouragement, self-love, empathy, and kindness to the young reader.

In the story, Hannah discovers that she is not alone by sharing her mental health struggles with a trusted, grown-up friend, and there are many helpful ways to feel better. Hannah becomes more confident and empowered by sharing her troubles with a caring adult team who expeditiously responds to Hannah with empathy, compassion, and kindness. The book clearly explains common symptoms and interventions regarding mental health issues. It is written and illustrated in inclusive, child-friendly terms emphasizing self-love and kindness and removing the stigmas associated with mental illness. Unique graphic designs merging real-life photographic images with colorful and animated illustrations offer special interests and invite opportunities for engagement throughout the story for the young reader. The book includes an invitation from Hannah's little dog, "MacKzie," to join Hannah and her friends in taking Hannah's "BE KIND TO YOUR MIND" Mental Health Pledge. The pledge reiterates the importance of sharing mental health problems, offers reassurance of available and unbiased help, and encourages healthy self-esteem through self-care.

The book integrates relevant child literacy with healthy mind concepts. It is written in accessible language for easy, age-appropriate mental health information. The "end rhymes" format is a building tool for healthy self-esteem. It supports children in early reading ventures with fun, rhythmic reading and matching illustrations to increase their confidence and enjoyment. The lightheartedness of child-friendly rhymes also offers the young reader a reprieve from the heaviness that can be associated with the subject of mental illness.

"Sometimes…Minds Get Boo-Boos, Too" may be a helpful resource to parents, caregivers, teachers, and counselors in assisting children experiencing mental health difficulties and as a lesson of empathy and inclusion for all children.

Carolyn Hunter, aka "Miss Cee Cee"

Author's Page

Hello! My name is Carolyn Hunter; children call me "Miss Cee Cee." My many hats include native Washingtonian, Daughter, Sister, Wife, Mother, Mimi, Early Childhood Educator, Kindness Influencer, Dog Mom, Social Media Blogger, and the Children's Book Author-Illustrator of "Mean, Mean COVID-19," "COVID-19 meets THE VACCINE," and "Sometimes…Minds Get Boo-Boos, Too." The John Hopkins Children's Center Pediatric COVID Vaccine Studies features my two COVID children's books. My book "COVID-19 meets the VACCINE" earned an honorary bookplate and is placed on the bookshelves of the National Library of Medicine.

I am committed to mentoring children through messages of kindness, as I believe kindness is a superpower with the potential to dwell within all of us to make the world a better place. My mantra is to "Love God, Self, and Others through Kindness." My sincere love for children infuses my passion for writing and illustrating books that educate, engage, and empower children to pursue their highest level of imagination. I am dedicated to assisting children with life lessons by improving critical thinking and problem-solving skills, building a positive self-image, healthy self-esteem, and inclusion through messages of kindness for self and others. I hope today's children who read and hear my storybooks will emulate what they've learned in their adult tomorrows and infiltrate the world with good deeds from good seeds birthed through "Cee Cee's Heart…where Kindness lives."

Carolyn Hunter

CeeCeesHeart.com
Carolyn@ceeceesheart.com

Acknowledgements

To my husband, Michael, thank you for all your love and support and for believing in me.

For our children, Ashley, Bria, Carlie, and Ian. For our grandchildren, Aiden, Nia, Carter, Noor, and Ariana; even our future grands. I hope my books remind you that your purpose is connected to your passion; embrace them both. I love you.

My extended family and friends, thank you for your continued love and support. You have cheered me on through another book, and I love you all!

To my Creative Designer, Caroll Atkins, thank you for stretching me beyond where I thought I could venture creatively. This experience was quite an adventure, and I look forward to many more with you!

To Dr. Susan Francis of Lavi Psychotherapy, your creditials in the field of mental health are highly esteemed. Your acceptance and approval of my intention to normalize mental health and encourage a culture where all children experience, reliable and trustworthy adult intervention, inclusion, and kindness for their mental well-being, is one of the highest honors of my life and confirmation of my purpose. Thank you.

To my cousin, Stephanie Page-Baxter. Your Masters Degree in Curriculum and Development coupled with 34 years of teaching expertise and dedication in Childhood Education, makes you and your guidance throughout this journey a godsend. Thank you so much for all your love and support.

To my little doggy companion and kindness partner, "MacKzie". Your beautiful heart is a blessing to so many. Thank you for "presenting" the story to children with such softness and care. I love you.

For every child that has cried silent tears, as I created this storybook, I felt your sadness; Miss Cee Cee loves you. May this book be a bridge to happier times.

For the "Hannah" who lives inside the hearts and minds of children, all grown up, be encouraged, and may peace be with you.

Pull up a chair; I have a story to tell,
About a little girl, Hannah, who didn't feel well.
I can tell the whole story, from beginning to end.
I'm her little dog MacKzie, and Hannah's best friend.

Was it a headache

or... sore toe that made her moan?

Was it a terrible toothache that made her groan?

No, none of these things were the reasons why,
Hannah felt sad and wanted to cry.
Her hurt was hidden and not easy to find,
Because it was deep inside of Hannah's mind.

The mind is where our thoughts live and grow,
It's the treasure chest that holds all we know.
Like dreams and memories of people, places, and things,
And the beautiful birdsong that the nightingale sings.

But all thoughts aren't happy ones,
Some make us frown,
While some thoughts lift our spirits up,

Others bring them down.

Our minds help paint the picture of how things make us feel
And hold our many countless thoughts, some pretend,
And sometimes real.

They are the superheroes of what we think and do,
Our minds achieve most any task that we put them to!

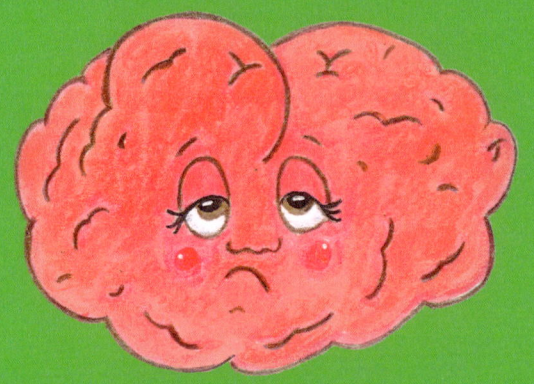

But sometimes our minds get tired

and sad,

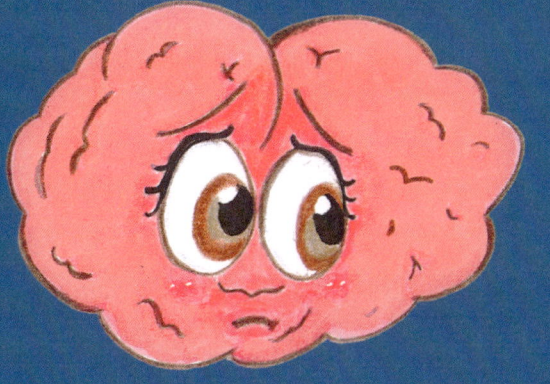

Sometimes our minds get fearful

or mad.

We can scrape our knees or bite our tongue when we chew,
But did you know,
Sometimes...Minds Get Boo-Boos, Too?

Or...
Make us afraid and want to hide
from unhappy feelings we hold inside.

Like, when someone we love has to go away,
And we'll miss them terribly and wish they'd stay.

When new things make us nervous
Or feel very strange,
Because our minds sometimes struggle,
Getting used to a change.

Or, when grown-ups around us have a misunderstanding,
And their voices get loud and sometimes demanding.

When bullies make it hard to like going to school,
Because they're tricked into thinking being mean
Makes them cool.

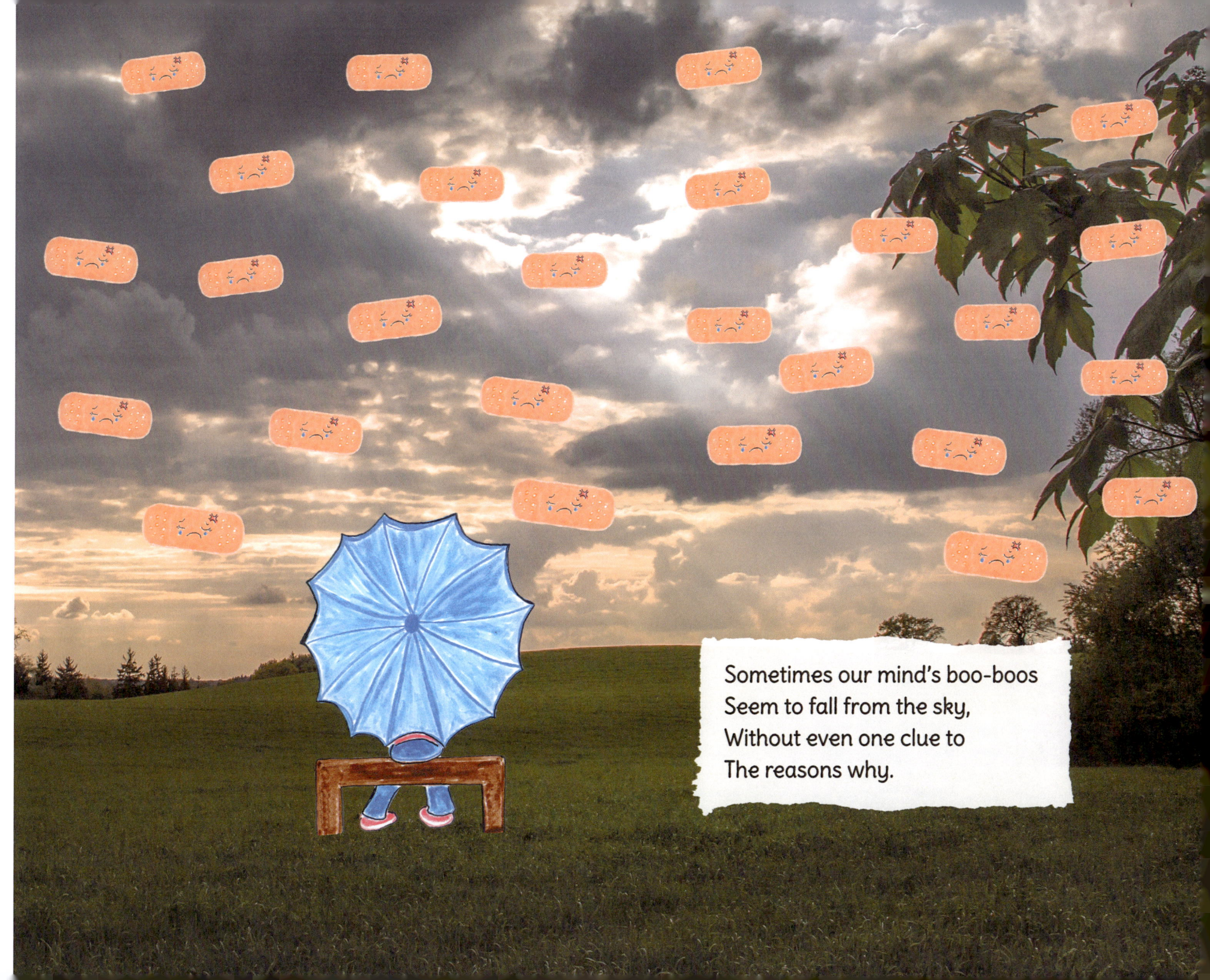
Sometimes our mind's boo-boos
Seem to fall from the sky,
Without even one clue to
The reasons why.

Hannah feared people would be unkind,
And laugh at the boo-boos inside her mind.
So she boxed them all up and put them high on a shelf,
And kept her sad feelings all to herself.

Like broken crayons being tossed to the ground,
She felt all mixed up and upside down
Hannah looked in the mirror and stared for a while,
It seemed her mind's boo-boos had run off with her smile.

It wouldn't be a secret,
For goodness' sake,
If Hannah took a fall
That made her funny bone break.

None of these things would make Hannah NOT tell,
A grown-up friend,
That she didn't feel well.
There's no good reason she could ever find,
To keep secrets about "owies,"
In her mind.

After all, our minds are part of our bodies too,
So they need the same care as our other parts do.

But we don't have to run and hide
Or keep our feelings bottled up inside:
Because our awesomeness sticks to us like glue,
No matter what part of us has a boo-boo!

When Hannah began to share her troubles,

Hannah discovered as she decided to share,
There were many kind helpers
To show her they care.

As she took her boo-boos off that shelf,
No longer keeping them to herself,
Hannah realized her mind needs care too,
Just as much as her other parts do;
Because Sometimes...Minds Get Boo-Boos, Too.

Hannah learned to feel better by having a talk,

Or from the exercise of an afternoon walk.

Or help from our doctors, who may give medication.

Hannah discovered there are many great ways,
For her to feel better
And have brighter days.

And just like Hannah, you now know too,
Never be ashamed of what's troubling you.
Just as towards others, we should always be kind,
We must be kind to ourselves, including our mind.

The story has come to an end,
But there's still one thing left to do.

Hannah and her friends took her Healthy Mind Pledge,
And invite you to take it too!

Julie

Malik

Hannah

Caleb

Lucy

Ryan

HANNAH'S HEALTHY MIND PLEDGE

I pledge to take care of my body,
Even the parts I cannot see.
I promise to always BE KIND TO MY MIND,
For it, too, is a part of me.
Asking for help from a grown-up friend,
Is a brave and smart thing to do.
Because they understand, just like me,
Sometimes...Minds Get Boo-Boos, Too.

Ana

Zara

Noah

Miya

Tyler

Ella

www.ingramcontent.com/pod-product-compliance
Lightning Source LLC
Chambersburg PA
CBRC101245160426
43209CB00025B/1894